6·29

ZP104

Marketing
in a week

ERIC DAVIES
BARRY DAVIES

Hodder & Stoughton

A MEMBER OF THE HODDER HEADLINE GROUP

Acknowledgements

The table on page 45 is reprinted with permission of Merrill, an imprint of Macmillan Publishing Company, from Marketing Research by Dodge, Fullerton and Rink. Copyright © 1982 Bell & Howell Company.

Orders: please contact Bookpoint Ltd, 130 Milton Park, Abingdon, Oxon OX14 4SB. Telephone: (44) 01235 827720. Fax: (44) 01235 400454. Lines are open from 9.00–6.00, Monday to Saturday, with a 24 hour message answering service. Email address: *orders@bookpoint.co.uk*

British Library Cataloguing in Publication Data
A catalogue record for this title is available from the British Library

ISBN 0 340 84955X

First published 1992
Impression number 10 9 8 7 6 5 4 3 2
Year   2007 2006 2005 2004 2003

Cover image: FPG/Getty Images

Printed in Great Britain for Hodder & Stoughton Educational, a division of Hodder Headline Plc, 338 Euston Road, London NW1 3BH by Cox & Wyman Ltd., Reading.

The leading organisation for professional management

As the champion of management, the Chartered Management Institute shapes and supports the managers of tomorrow. By sharing intelligent insights and setting standards in management development, the Institute helps to deliver results in a dynamic world.

Setting and raising standards

The Institute is a nationally accredited organisation, responsible for setting standards in management and recognising excellence through the award of professional qualifications.

Encouraging development, improving performance

The Institute has a vast range of development programmes, qualifications, information resources and career guidance to help managers and their organisations meet new challenges in a fast-changing environment.

Shaping opinion

With in-depth research and regular policy surveys of its 91,000 individual members and 520 corporate members, the Chartered Management Institute has a deep understanding of the key issues. Its view is informed, intelligent and respected.

For more information call 01536 204222 or visit www.managers.org.uk

■■■■ C O N T E N T S ■■■■

Eric Davies BA, MPhil, DipM, is Director of Research and Strategy at Ontrac: Communication.

Eric is a member of the Industrial Marketing Research Association, the Marketing Education Group, an Associate of the Institute of Management Consultants and holds the Diploma of the Institute of Marketing. His consulting experience has covered a wide range of areas including management training for the Chartered Management Institute.

Eric has contributed articles to the *European Journal of Marketing, Accountancy, The Pakistan Management Review* and *Municipal Journal*, to name but a few.

Barry Davies DMS, MA, is Professor of Marketing at Cheltenham and Gloucester College of Higher Education.

Barry has lectured and consulted widely, including periods researching at Cranfield School of Management and the Polytechnics of Wales and Manchester. His main interests are in marketing strategy and policy, particularly in the area of services.

Barry's commercial experience includes posts in the retail cooperative movement and general management in the vending and industrial catering sectors.

There are many factors that influence the success of a business, but it must be true that customers are **the** most important factor. Without customers the business has no purpose and ultimately will cease to exist. Winning customers, therefore, is a critical business activity. Before we can use all the other resources and skills in the business we have to have customers.

Marketing is about winning and retaining customers. Businesses win customers by satisfying their needs in a way that the customer perceives to be better than other suppliers. The process of satisfying customers' needs is directly related to achieving the goals of the business.

Today we are going to take an overview of marketing. This overview will be sub-divided into four sections:

1 Definition of marketing (the marketing orientation)
2 Why adopt a marketing orientation?
3 Marketing and sales
4 Marketing and the company

These four sections outline why every business should adopt the marketing approach.

Definition of marketing

'Marketing is the identification and profitable satisfaction of customers' needs'

A firm's profits, indeed its very survival, depend on the satisfaction of its customers' needs. This very simplicity makes marketing a subtle concept and one which is difficult to make operational.

Marketing has three components:

- Identifying needs
- Satisfying them
- Making a profit

You could say there is a *matching* process in operation, i.e. that of matching the company's capabilities to the wants of its customers. But remember, whether or not a formalised matching process is instituted, for a firm to be profitable, some sort of match must exist.

Over the years, some business people have been able to develop very successful, 'intuitive' matching.

So what is the point of marketing at all? The answer lies in the nature of the modern business environment. Today, companies face a complex and rapidly changing environment. One wrong decision, or misallocated resource, could spell disaster: Today's business environment is one of high risk.

> Marketing, therefore, is concerned with attempting to reduce risk by systematically applying formal techniques to assess the situation and develop the company's response to it.

Why adopt a marketing orientation?

Simply because marketing makes a firm more profitable!

You must be saying, 'Well, they would say that wouldn't they!'. But you don't have to believe *us*. Have a look at Figure 1 which is drawn from a major UK study of marketing practice. Basically, the bar chart shows the breakdown of the sample (some 1700 companies) by 'orientation' (i.e. how they approach their business) and profit performance.

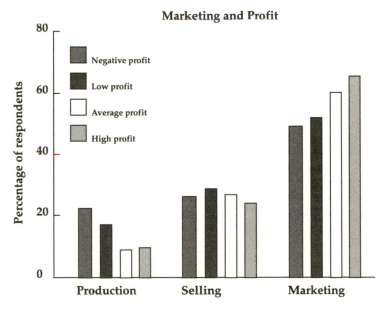

FIGURE 1 *Marketing and Profit*

You will notice that the marketing oriented firms are skewed to the high profit band. If company orientation had no effect on profit then each of the three orientations should display similar distributions. This seems to suggest that a marketing orientation enhances profitability (while a production orientation depresses it).

This is very important; marketing is relevant to the most basic business objective, i.e. profit and it is worth the attention of any manager who is interested in improving his or her performance.

Marketing and sales

Marketing is *not* an American word for selling and selling is not the same as marketing.

Selling is simply that part of marketing concerned with persuading customers to acquire the product or service which best matches the organisation's capabilities with its customers' wants.

If the marketing job has been done well, such selling may still be tough, but it will be effective. If not, salesmen all too often find themselves trying to sell what the producing organisation wants the customer to want, i.e. not necessarily what the customer actually wants. This is very important, because although a customer may be persuaded to buy a product once, to develop repeat purchases the product must satisfy the customer's needs precisely.

Selling, then, is the *last* stage in the marketing process.

Marketing and the company

There seem to be four factors which influence success. Researchers have presented these factors as the 'virtuous circle of best marketing practice' as shown in Figure 2.

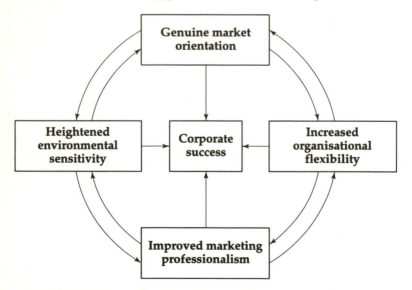

FIGURE 2 *The Virtuous Circle of Best Marketing Practice*

The 'virtuous circle of best marketing practice' is made up of four major elements:

- *Genuine market orientation* – the identification and satisfaction of customers' needs.
- *Heightened environmental sensitivity* – a commitment to monitoring, scanning and assessing changes in the marketplace.
- *Organisational flexibility and adaptability* – the need to avoid an over-rigid structure within the company and a mechanism for changing this structure in line with changes in the environment.
- *Increased marketing professionalism* – a commitment to the recruitment of trained marketing professionals and the realisation of the benefits of on-going training.

Summary

Marketing can be defined as 'the identification and profitable satisfaction of customers' needs'. There are three elements to this definition: identifying needs, satisfying them and making a profit.

You could say marketing is a 'matching' process – matching the capabilities of the company to the wants of its customers. Marketing is important to managers because it has a beneficial impact on company profitability.

Marketing is not an American word for selling. Selling is the last stage of the marketing process.

The research seems to suggest that a marketing oriented company is likely to be more successful because of four major factors:

- The company is *genuinely* marketing oriented (not just saying they are marketing oriented)
- They are sensitive to the environment in which they operate. They monitor customer attitudes, competitive action, changes in society, the economy, legislation, etc.
- They have flexible organisations that can adapt to meet the changing needs of the market
- Their staff demonstrate increased marketing professionalism – employing trained marketing professionals and acknowledging the benefits of on-going training

Today we are going to look at the 'nuts and bolts' of marketing. We are going to introduce the marketing decision process and consider marketing planning. This chapter will be sub-divided into:

1 The marketing decision process
2 Setting objectives
3 The marketing planning cycle
   3.1 SWOT
   3.2 Plan
   3.3 Implement
   3.4 Control

The marketing decision process

Marketing is very much about making decisions which are inter-related, e.g. 'Which part of the market are we going to target on?', 'What will we say in our advertisement?', 'Where will we advertise?' or 'What price will we charge?'.

Clearly, it is important to set up a hierarchy of decision making which puts each decision area in an appropriate order – this is the 'marketing decision process'.

It is called a process because it starts from the beginning, 'objectives', and moves, systematically, through to 'tactics', the detail of marketing activity – this has been simplified in Figure 3.

OBJECTIVES
|
THE MARKET
|
MARKET SEGMENTS
|
THE TARGET
|
THE NEEDS/WANTS/DESIRES
|
EXTERNAL ATTITUDE INFLUENCES
|
THE BENEFITS
|
THE COMPETITION
|
THE STRATEGY

Components:

'THE MARKETING MIX'

PRODUCT
PRICE
DISTRIBUTION
PROMOTION

TACTICS
|
REVIEW

FIGURE 3 *The Marketing Decision Process*

Unfortunately, many business people assume that the detail of tactical marketing is the area to concentrate on. They enthusiastically place advertisements in all sorts of publications, without giving any thought to the customers they are trying to reach, what their needs are, what sort of message will influence them, or where they are likely to be found.

Advertising, particularly, is the glossy end of marketing, but remember that for every successful advertising campaign there is a vast amount of planning effort, using research, perhaps test marketing and many other tools in order to achieve this level of success. In fact, an effective advertisement is the tip of the marketing iceberg!

The rest of the book follows the stages of the marketing decision process.

Setting objectives

It is necessary for a business to establish a list of objectives so that strategy can be drafted to achieve these objectives. These can be *economic*, e.g. return on investment, or sales targets (i.e. quantitative); or they can be *non-economic*, e.g. reduce owner's involvement (i.e. qualitative). Objectives can also be *defensive*, e.g. improving cash flow. Strategy development is pointless unless a clear statement of objectives is made: if we don't know where we want to go, how can we get there?

Objectives should be translated into annual targets and, therefore, a short-/medium-term plan. However, it is unrealistic to set targets without considering the marketplace. Clearly, it is important for a firm to match its strengths to opportunities in the marketplace. The mechanism for accomplishing this is known as 'marketing planning'.

Marketing planning can be defined as 'anticipatory decision making'.

Confucius wrote 'If a man gives no thought to distant things, he will find sorrow near at hand'. This remark encapsulates the bed-rock reason for planning: planning helps avoid failure by forcing the manager to consider the objectives, his or her organisation and the environment.

The marketing planning cycle

Planning can be represented as a 'cycle', as shown in
Figure 4.

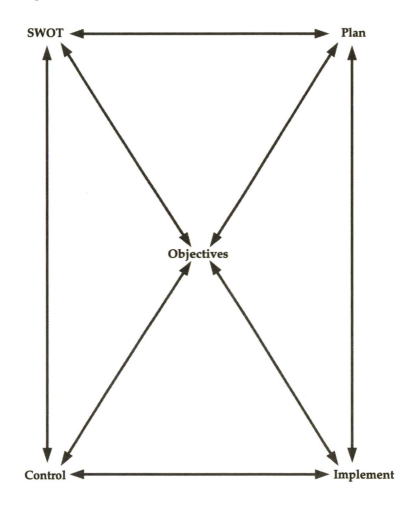

FIGURE 4 *The Marketing Planning Cycle*

The motto is: 'Work the plan and plan the work'.

> *The Marketing Planning Cycle*
>
> 1 SWOT
> 2 Plan
> 3 Implement
> 4 Control

SWOT

This stage of the process of planning is focused on providing answers to the question 'Where are we now?'. In some organisations, this question will require wide-ranging answers which dwell at length on outside (external) factors. Such wide-ranging answers may consider in detail society's and the government's expectations of business. More generally, companies often find that the two external groups which need to be studied are customers and competitors. These two groups are central to the *external* audit.

In contrast, the *internal* audit examines the company's own resources, and supplies suggestions as to company strengths and weaknesses. Putting internal and external audit results together produces a SWOT analysis – the *strengths* and *weaknesses* of the firm and the *opportunities* and *threats* in the environment.

To complete a successful SWOT analysis requires a good database. If facts are not available, the firm must take steps to get them and they must be objective. There are two tools commonly used in SWOT analysis.

- The management audit (internal)
- Marketing research (external) – this topic is covered below

Once the database has been assembled, the SWOT analysis can be conducted. One way of looking at SWOT analysis is to consider it as a planning 'balance sheet'.

Within the company		In the environment	
Strengths	+	Opportunities	+
Weaknesses	–	Threats	–

FIGURE 5 *The Planning Balance Sheet*

Within the company, managers will focus on maintaining and enhancing strengths, whilst addressing weaknesses. In the business environment, managers will seek to exploit opportunities and minimise the impact of threats on their business.

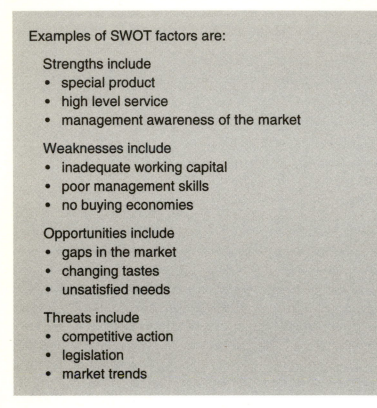

Examples of SWOT factors are:

Strengths include
- special product
- high level service
- management awareness of the market

Weaknesses include
- inadequate working capital
- poor management skills
- no buying economies

Opportunities include
- gaps in the market
- changing tastes
- unsatisfied needs

Threats include
- competitive action
- legislation
- market trends

It is worth remembering that a threat can be turned into an opportunity; indeed, it has been said that a threat is merely an opportunity in disguise.

If a firm completes its SWOT analysis properly, it will be in a much better position to make strategic decisions, because information reduces risk in decision-making.

Plan

Many marketing writers have looked at particular tools which aid planning. Probably the major problem for firms in today's dynamic markets is the management of product portfolios: i.e. the balance of mature products with declining products and new products. There are two famous tools worth considering – the *Boston box* and the *product life cycle.*

The Boston box
Perhaps the most widely known of the product/market strategy tools is the Boston Consulting Group's original growth/share matrix, (or Boston box) as presented in Figure 6 below:

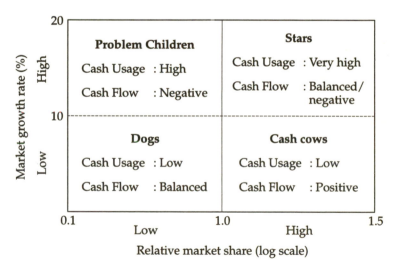

FIGURE 6 *The Boston Box*

There are a number of features in this deceptively simple matrix. The edges of the matrix are scales measuring values which many companies know – growth rates for particular product markets in real terms (the vertical axis), and relative market share (on the bottom axis).

Relative market share is a measure of a product's market share in relation to the share of the market leader. A relative market share of 0.5 would mean that the company's product had a market share half the size of the market leader; a relative market share of 1.5 would indicate the company's product had a market share of one and a half times the nearest competitor. Scores of below 1.0 indicate that the company is not the market leader, of 1.0 or above that it is the market leader.

In general, a marketing rule of thumb (supported by research) is that high market share leads to high profitability (in the medium-term plus). High market share is thus seen as desirable but this may conflict with short-term accounting views.

A company should seek to balance its portfolio of products. It will need future 'cash cows' which may be today's 'stars': 'dogs' in today's portfolio require active decisions – is there potential for turning into cash cows, or should they be 'put down'? Can 'problem children' be turned into 'stars'?

There are perhaps four types of unbalanced product portfolio. The table below shows these types and the typical corporate symptoms to which they give rise.

Basic Problem	Typical Symptoms
Too many dogs	Inadequate cash flow
	Inadequate profits
	Inadequate growth
Too many problem children	Inadequate cash flow
	Inadequate profits
Too many cash cows	Inadequate growth
	Excessive cash flow in the relatively short-term
	Little opportunity for investment/growth
Too many stars	Excessive cash needs
	Excessive management demands
	Unstable growth and profits

The product life cycle

The second tool is the product life cycle (PLC). A typical product life cycle is presented in Figure 7.

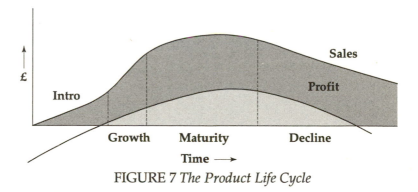

FIGURE 7 *The Product Life Cycle*

The four stages shown (introduction, growth, maturity, decline) are fairly arbitrarily designated. In some product categories studies have supported the idea of PLC – particularly for some grocery brands. It may be harder to determine PLCs for generic product types (motor cars) than for particular brands (Austin Allegro).

The PLC is an idea which is intuitively attractive. However, it may be very difficult to position products/brands on it. In such situations, PLCs might serve as a focus for thinking.

This table shows the chief effects of the product life cycle:

Characteristics of:	Introduction	Growth	Maturity	Decline
• Sales	Low	Fast rise	Slow rise	Decline
• Profits	Negligible	Peak	Decline	Low/nil
• Cash flow	Negative	Moderate	High	Low
• Customers	Innovators	Early adopters	Late adopters	Laggards
• Competitors	Few	Growing	Many	Fewer
Firm responses:				
• Strategic focus	Market expansion	Market penetration	Defend share	Product-ivity
• Marketing expenditure	High	High (lower %)	Falling	Low
• Marketing emphasis	Awareness	Brand preference	Brand loyalty	Selective
Price	High	Lower	Lowest	Rising
Product	Basic	Improved	Different-iated	Rational-ised

Source: 'The realities of the product life cycle' by Peter Doyle, *Quarterly Review of Marketing* (Summer 1976)

The above tools are merely aids to management in terms of the way they think about their planning options. Once decisions have been made, based on SWOT and (where appropriate) consideration of the insights stemming from particular tools, a plan must be drafted.

It is important to keep plans:

- Appropriate – Is this *what* I need to know?
- Complete – Is this *all* I need to know?
- Specific – Can I *action* this plan?
- Adaptable – What about *monitoring* and *contingencies*?

Implement

To implement the plan we will need to:

- Select operational variables
- Establish time limits and deadlines
- Communicate and assign tasks
- Develop sales forecasts
- Monitor the environment for variations from planning assumptions
- Determine action plans for individuals
- Set sales quotas
- Prepare budgets

Control

The choice of operational variables above gives rise to the *control data*. The chosen variables must be monitored against planned figures to give a basis for managerial action. At the same time, the environment is scanned to watch for disturbances outside the assumptions underlying the plan. The techniques to be employed are those familiar from the budgeting area: a watch for variances and the instigation of corrective actions.

Finally

Planning is a process simple to describe but extremely difficult to implement. In general terms, the plan may be seen as directed towards securing some competitive advantage. The PIMS (Profit Impact of Marketing Strategy) on-going study indicates that companies adopting a formal marketing approach out-perform competitors in the same industry who do not. Other research studies support this view – planning for competitive advantage pays.

Marketing planning is an on-going process – it is not a large report left in the bottom drawer of the filing cabinet. Managers must seek to minimise subjective evaluations; and the firm must be 'environmentally sensitive' and internally adaptable.

Planning is only one element in running a successful business, but a key one. The plan and the process of planning lend cohesion, direction and thrust to the enterprise. Planning focuses on objectives and goals and stimulates heightened motivation *if the organisational climate is right*.

Summary

The Marketing Decision Process is a series of decision areas that need to be considered when developing a marketing strategy. The process attempts to offer a 'systematic' approach to marketing decision making, starting with setting 'objectives' and moving through to 'tactics'.

Clearly, in defining company objectives it is important to match the company's strengths to opportunities in the marketplace. This is known as Marketing Planning. Planning helps to avoid failure by forcing the manager to consider the objectives, his/her organisation and the environment. The planning cycle is made up of four stages:

- SWOT – establishing the strengths and weaknesses of the company (internal) and the opportunities and threats (external) in the environment
- Plan – drafting appropriate, complete, specific and adaptable plans
- Implementation – as for all team activities, consideration must be given to operational variables, e.g. sales goals, action plans, assignment of tasks, time limits, feedback, etc.
- Control – the comparison of 'actual' to 'budget' and feedback into the planning and implementation stages

Planning is easier to talk about than to do. But when there is appropriate determination on the part of managers, effective plans can be developed. Remember the process of planning (i.e. starting with SWOT and following the stages of the cycle) is more important than formal written plans that may be out of date before they are used.

Today we are going to look at the next three elements of the marketing decision process:

- The market
- The market segments
- Targets

Have another look at the model (Figure 3, page 16) to refresh your memory.

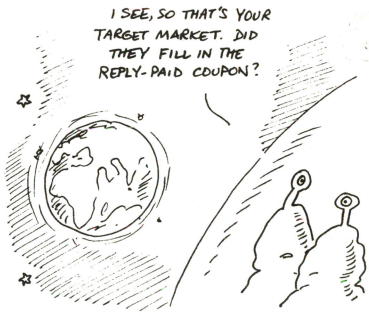

The market

We are now concerned with the overall market: its shape, conduct and peculiarities. There is frequent confusion about the total market for a particular product. The total market is the total amount spent in the satisfaction of a need, irrespective of the products which satisfy that need.

Take for instance, the 'clean clothes market'. This market will include three basic types of product offer:

- In-home cleaning and washing
- Out of home cleaning and washing, e.g dry cleaning
- Disposable clothes, e.g. disposable nappies

If we take the first of these types of product offer, (remembering here that 'product' refers to the benefit sought, i.e. a physical product or a service) then in home clothes cleaning and washing would probably be further broken down into:

- Employing someone in the home to undertake the tasks
- Using home laundry appliances to ease the task undertaken by household members e.g. washing machines, tumble dryers, etc.
- Using household members' labour only

The first task is, therefore, to assess the total **market worth**, i.e. the total financial value of consumption. Secondly, the nature of the growth of this demand must be reviewed.

We need to find out what were the shares of the market held by each product type and what were the trends in each over the last, say, four years. If the product type that your firm makes is in decline, whilst competitors' products are in growth, this could pose a threat to the success of your company.

The market segments

Every market can be segmented into groups of potential customers who have similar characteristics. The benefit to the marketer in doing this is that each segment has less variability in it than the market as a whole. Therefore, we can expect customers within a segment to have broadly similar needs.

There are four requirements for effective segmentation:

1   For a segment to be isolated from other segments, customers within that segment must be different from customers in other segments on some dimension/s and must be similar to each other within the segment.

2   The criteria used to segment the market must be based on differences in customer demand relevant to the purchase situation i.e. different segments have different hierarchies of needs.

3   The segment must be of sufficient potential size to ensure an adequate return on marketing investment.

4   An identified market segment can only be exploited if it can be reached. It must be possible to direct a separate marketing strategy (mix) to each segment.

Returning to the 'clean clothes' example, there are probably three broad 'customer' segments:

• Domestic i.e. individuals/households
• Commercial i.e. hotels, pubs, retailers (for uniforms)
• Industrial i.e. factories (for overalls)

There may be a further segmentation of groups two and three by size of operation, and of group one by socio-economic group and perhaps location.

The target

At this stage, it is necessary to consider, as systematically as possible, all the available segments and rank them in terms of their fit to the strengths and weaknesses of the firm and the objectives of the management.

However, it is important to consider the positioning of the competition (see below).

Figure 8 shows a convenient way to look at this.

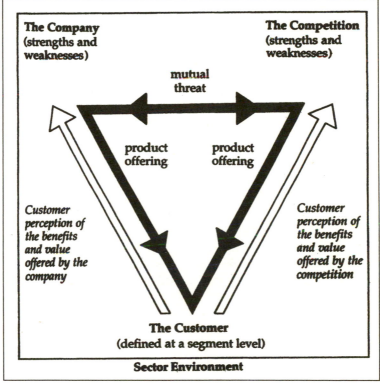

FIGURE 8 *The 3 Cs Triangle*

In some senses, the '3 Cs' triangle has echoes of concepts which we have already considered – both SWOT analysis and segmentation strategy are related to it. The basic idea of the 3 Cs triangle is very simple – what is difficult, is holding a broad vision when confronted with a mass of detail.

The main idea is that the company needs to review its strengths and weaknesses objectively in relation to the opportunities provided by the customer (or client) and to assess the competition's relative position.

In its simplest terms, marketing is a matching process – matching the company's strengths to opportunities amongst customers, whilst recognising the competition's positioning. In essence, this is the 3 Cs triangle.

The process of developing a strategy through the 3 Cs is as follows:

Company
1   What are our strengths and weaknesses in the marketing sense?

2   What are the corporate objectives and are they realistic given the opportunities and threats in the market place?

Customer
1   Do the customers perceive our strengths (as translated into benefits) to be appropriate to their needs?

2   Do particular groups (segments) of customers have a higher propensity (than average for all other customers) to require these benefits, i.e. are they the best target?

Competition
1   Who are our direct competitors? What are their profiles, e.g. scale, financial position, marketing strategy, market positioning?

2   How do the customers perceive the competition's offerings? Do they think our competitor's offerings have more or fewer benefits, appropriate to their needs, than ours?

This is where the matching process comes in.

Clearly, it is necessary to assess each group of customers and to rank the segments in terms of our company's strengths and weaknesses and the competition's strengths and weaknesses.

Having ranked the segments in terms of the match between segment requirements, company capabilities and competitive offerings, then a strategy focused on those segments showing the best fit should offer the greatest promise of success.

Summary

Often the starting point in developing a marketing strategy is the need to define the market. The 'total' market for a product or service is the total amount spent in the satisfaction of a need, irrespective of the products/services which satisfy that need. Often marketing research is used to make value definitions of total market worth.

All markets can be broken down into market segments. Segments can be defined as sub-groups of the market that show similar needs within the segment compared to the market as a whole.

Targeting is concerned with identifying the segment (or segments) that offer the best return on effort for the company, i.e. to match the company's strengths to opportunities offered by the segments whilst minimising the threats posed by the competition.

On Tuesday we considered a very important aspect of marketing decision making – the process of identifying the best target for our firm. Implicit in the approach described on Tuesday is the availability of objective information about markets and segments. Today, we are going to look at the way such information is obtained, i.e. marketing research.

Marketing research

Marketing research (MR) is:

'The systematic gathering, recording and analysing of data about problems relating to the marketing of goods and services.'

Source: *American Marketing Association*

Executives need information to reduce risk in decision making. Marketing research is a tool of management, its function is to provide answers to questions important to management in discharging their duties. Whilst risk can never be eliminated in business decision making, it can be reduced by using the market research process.

The five steps of marketing research

Marketing research can be broken down into five steps, as follows:

Step 1   Problem identification
Step 2   Secondary research
Step 3   Primary research
Step 4   Analysis and interpretation
Step 5   Using the results

Step 1

The definition of the problem is the most important element in marketing research. There is a saying:

'A problem well defined is a problem half solved.'

Normally, the problem manifests itself in a list of 'need-to-know' pieces of information, i.e. information necessary to make a sector informed decision. It is important that due consideration is given to this stage, to ensure that the research is pertinent and useful to the management's decision problem.

There may be two basic problem forms:

- The problem of exploiting an opportunity
- Overcoming an obstacle

Problem definition consists of a series of steps:
1 Recognising the problem situation
2 Examining the symptoms
3 Defining the problem
4 Research objective/s (or the research brief)

A problem develops out of a lack of information regarding the possible determinants of a range of strategic actions, e.g. market worth, trends, competitive offerings, price value perceptions, customers' attitudes/behaviour, etc.

Step 2
Secondary or desk research is concerned with reviewing secondary data, i.e. data which is collected by other people for purposes other than those specific to the problem in hand. There are two basic sources:

- Internal, i.e. within the firm, and
- External, i.e. from outside organisations, including the government, academic institutions and authors, and commercial sources, including 'on line' sources

Probably the major source of secondary data is the government.

Sources can include:

- Government statistics – product data, market trends, etc.
- Commercial research data – e.g. 'Mintel' product reports
- Academic research data – sourced through the Directory of Academic Research

- Lists – trade directories, specialist list builders
- Company performance – Companies House for searches and ratio analysis, e.g. ICC

The advantages of desk research are:
1 An abundance of data may save the researcher considerable time and money
2 The detailed research brief for the field research can be better defined
3 Some secondary sources could not be replicated by any one organisation, e.g. The Census

The disadvantages are:
1 Assessing the degree of accuracy of the data, i.e. how was it gathered, analysed, interpreted and presented?
2 The data may be too old, i.e. gathered many years ago and therefore not of use now
3 The data may be irrelevant to the problem in hand

Data from desk research can give the firm information to assess opportunities and threats in the marketplace.

However, often there is a need for further data to:

- Answer questions unanswered by desk research
- Answer questions to facilitate the drafting and implementation of marketing strategies

Step 3

Field (or primary) research is concerned with the collection of data directly from the market. Field research techniques draw heavily on statistics, survey methods, social psychology and marketing theory.

There are three key areas in field research:

(i)   Interviewing techniques

There are three basic interviewing* techniques:

(a)   Face-to-face
(b)   Telephone
(c)   Direct mail

(a)   This technique involves direct interviewing, either using a fully-structured or a semi-structured questionnaire. It is a versatile and productive interviewing technique allowing the interviewer to probe the respondent on particular points.
      However, this same personal interaction can lead to problems of bias.
      Also, this technique is expensive both in terms of interviewer time and expenses.

* Remember that observation is a further method of collecting marketing information

(b)   This technique uses the telephone as a medium for direct questioning. The method allows fast collection of data over a wide geographical area. Expenses are significantly lower than face-to-face, and the interviewer can make a large number of interviews.

However, the tool is only applicable to situations where all the possible respondents (i.e. the sample frame) have a telephone and are available during the researcher's working period, or potential bias from contacting only telephone owners will give rise to results which can be 'corrected'.

Also, telephone interviews are normally much shorter than face-to-face and do not allow the same degree of flexibility and opportunities for probing.

(c) This technique involves sending a questionnaire to the respondents who then answer the questions and return the questionnaire to the researcher.

This is the cheapest form of gathering information. The respondent is able to complete the questionnaire at leisure, thereby improving accuracy.

The very anonymity of the tool breaks down the problem of interviewer bias, especially status bias.

However, the major disadvantage is the possibility of a low response and the resulting non-response error, i.e. people who do not respond may be expressing an opinion/attitude to the research area and therefore the responses received will be biased.

The following table ranks* interviewing techniques by feature:

	Cost	Versatility	Amount of information	Speed	Administration
Face-to-face	3	1	1	2	3
Telephone	2	2	2	1	1
Direct mail	1	3	3	3	2

Source: *Marketing Research* by Dodge, Fullerton and Rink (Merrill, 1982)

*Ranked from most advantageous (1) to least advantageous (3)

(ii)   Sampling techniques

Sampling involves taking a portion of a whole 'thing' (called a *target population*) so that estimates may be made about the certain characteristics for the whole, based on the occurrence of the characteristic in the sample.

The starting point is the definition of the target population – for instance the list of members of the Royal British Institute of Architects would provide a complete list of members or cases. Such a population list (i.e. all architects) is called the *sample* or *sampling frame.*

> The obvious reasons for sampling, rather than using the whole population, are to save cost and time.

The most important feature regarding sampling is that the sample should be representative of the population as a whole. If the population is totally homogeneous, i.e. every case is identical, then only one item need be sampled regardless of the size of the population. Unfortunately in marketing research this is never the case.

There are two basic types of sample:

- Probability (or random)
- Non-probability

In the case of probability sampling, each case has the same chance of selection and the findings can be presented quantitatively, e.g. '60 per cent of the sample like our product'. For managers, the key questions must be: 'How representative are the sample findings, compared to the population?' To answer this, we need to consider two statistical concepts:

1 *Allowable error*
   This is the difference between the results obtained from the sample, compared with the true value for the population. Normally, this is represented as plus or minus per cent i.e. 60 per cent like our product, plus or minus 2.5 per cent.

2. *Level of confidence*

   This is a measure of probability that the true value will fall within the interval, which is created by adding and subtracting the allowable error. This too, is normally expressed as a percentage. For most commercial research, a 95 per cent level of confidence is used. Researchers use a formula to set sample sizes which deliver findings within set levels of allowable error and level of confidence.

With non-probability sampling, the element of randomness is removed and 'judgement' sampling is used. Often this type of research is called 'qualitative' (i.e. rather than quantitative). Non-probability sampling can be used to deal with special populations where particular cases must be included or where 'depth' of information is needed.

Within each of these broad areas, there are further types of sampling, (e.g. stratified random sampling), relevant to particular research situations.

(iii)   Data collection techniques

The major data collection technique is the question. This seems simple enough. However, there is an art to questioning. The main way researchers gather information is through a questionnaire, i.e. a standardised form for collecting data, allowing the researcher to compare responses from all respondents on a structured and comparable basis.

The researcher is concerned with how the answers to each question will be used, to ensure that the required data are generated, i.e. answers to the 'need-to-know' questions.

The development of a good questionnaire is an *iterative* process, i.e. you need to do it many times and each time it gets better! Experience is, therefore, of primary importance, but there are two areas which are particularly important:

- Question content
- Structure of questions

The golden rule in question content is to keep the question direct. The following points are also worth noting:

- Use words which are understood by the respondent
- Avoid ambiguities
- Avoid leading the respondent
- Avoid pressurising the respondent
- Avoid adding unnecessary prestige bias to the question

The structure of the question determines how the respondent will answer. There are many different forms of structure – some of the most commonly used are:

- Open – The respondent can answer the question in his/
  her own words
- Dichotomous – Only alternatives, e.g. Yes/No
- Multiple Choice – Several options, including 'other,
  please state', allowing the respondents to add to the list
  of options if they feel it is incomplete
- Scales – Often used in attitudinal research. They are
  based on opposites, e.g. agree – disagree. Perhaps
  the most popular scale is the semantic differential. The
  scale is a series of categories with extremes defined in
  terms of bipolar adjectives, e.g. strong – weak

Step 4
Once the data have been collected it is necessary to analyse
them to make them more useful in terms of the objectives of

the research. Each stage of the research process is interdependent and the form of analysis should be decided prior to beginning the field work.

A vast number of statistical tests exist for analysing data. Also, there are several computer programmes available to execute analysis both on mainframe computers and micro-computers. One of the most powerful micro-computer programmes available is The Statistical Package for Social Scientists – PC (SPSS – PC) and is strongly recommended for applications involving more than simple data treatments.

It is extremely important that we appreciate the implications of a particular test. The golden rule is to keep the analysis as simple as possible. For example, percentages are valuable, so are simple cross tabulations, i.e. putting a variable like 'attitude' against a variable like 'age', to see if there are any differences in attitude based on the age of respondents.

Step 5
If the benefits of research are going to be reaped by the firm then it is essential that the information is used and not merely filed away. Research is, to an extent, an agent of change – it can result in either a revision of tactics, or, on a more fundamental level, a change in the strategy of the company. To return to Figure 2, heightened environmental sensitivity must be matched with increased organisational flexibility. In other words it must be accepted that the firm must change in response to a changing environment.

Summary

Central to defining the market, segmenting and targeting is the need for information to reduce risk in decision making. The tool that delivers this information is Marketing Research – it is defined as 'the systematic gathering, recording and analysing of data about problems relating to the marketing of goods and services'. There are five steps:

- Problem identification
- Secondary research (i.e. published sources)
- Primary research (i.e. using questionnaires and sampling, etc.)
- Analysis and interpretation (i.e. computer assisted techniques, etc.)
- Using the results – introducing the information into the Marketing Decision Process

Today we are going to look at customer needs, wants and desires, how external attitude influencers affect decisions, the importance of product benefits and understanding the competition.

Customer needs, wants and desires

We have touched on ways of identifying the needs held by the target groups, but let us put this problem in a broader context. All purchasing is driven by *motives*. There are five broad suggested levels of motive as defined by Maslow:

Level	Example
Physiological	hunger
Safety	danger avoidance
Love	giving and receiving
Esteem	respect of others
Self-actualisation	self-fulfilment

Every individual has a set of *attitudes* which influence how various motives manifest themselves. Part of this is the individual's image of him/herself.

If this *sounds* complicated, it's because it *is* complicated! Several leading marketing academics have applied themselves to developing models of consumer behaviour. However, for the purpose of this book, we are concerned simply with what the customer needs in terms of product features and characteristics, i.e. benefits.

We could imagine that consumers in the domestic market for, say tumble dryers (air vented: full size) would have the following needs:

- Capacity
- Performance (in drying time, evenness of drying, tangle-crease-free finish)
- Reliability
- Indicators and controls
- Convenience of use (e.g. ease of using vent hose, ease of cleaning)
- Child safety (i.e. stability of unit)
- Design aesthetics

But this list would have to be tested by research and modified as necessary and examined to determine which needs are the most important. If we know this we can develop benefits in the product appropriate to those customers' needs.

External influences on customers' attitudes

When an individual makes a buying decision he or she is influenced by the views and attitudes of others. These others may be within the buying 'unit' e.g. in the case of the family this may be your spouse, parents or children, or, in the case of a company it could be your colleagues, superiors or subordinates.

Also, influence can come from outside the buying unit. In many buying situations the views of 'significant others' have a marked effect on the purchase decision. Often an individual's friends can influence his or her decision (e.g. in buying a new washing machine).

Considering the purchase of a washing machine, for example, a person may seek a partner's opinion, or friends' opinions and probably take advice from the local retailer. He or she may also consult magazines such as *Which!*. The importance of any external attitude influence is dependent upon the personalities of the influencer and the buyer.

For instance, when buying a washing machine, Mr and Mrs Smith may be strongly influenced by their friends, Mr and Mrs Jones. They may value the Jones' opinions to such an extent that their purchasing decision is affected.

The situation which we are discussing is of major importance to the marketing of all goods and services. Probably the most graphic illustration is the personal selling situation. If you, as a sales person, understand how your prospective buyer will behave, you can increase the probability of making a successful sale. This means identifying who is the 'real' decision maker and offering benefits appropriate to that person's needs.

Benefits to customers

The customer has needs which are also influenced by other people. In general terms, most buyers develop a hierarchy of needs which range from 'most important' to 'least important'; e.g. to one customer group, design aesthetics will be more important than, say, performance. Quite clearly, the seller must have product benefits which satisfy these needs and must ensure that the relative importance of these needs are taken into consideration in the development of the strategy.

An advertisement listing a number of product features without attempting to relate them to the satisfaction of perceived customer needs is probably not an effective advertisement in the sense that it is not actually persuading customers that the product matches their needs.

Every individual develops a way of evaluating products in terms of value. Customers perceive that one product is better value than another for various reasons. 'Good value' can be defined as the collection of benefits relevant to a set of needs which can be bought for the lowest cost, i.e. given that all other product features are equal, then price is the only variable. However, in most cases, other product features are not equal. In such cases product prices can vary dramatically and different customers will perceive different products as being the 'best' value although the prices are vastly different.

To complicate the matter further, benefits can be sub-divided into:

- Tangible benefits
- Intangible benefits

Tangible benefits are the things which are directly accessible to our senses; intangible benefits are those feelings we have about products which can come from many different sources. By assessing the package of benefits in a product a customer can make decisions regarding *value*. In other words the customer can perform a benefit/cost trade off.

The price band for motor cars probably goes from £5000 to £500 000. It seems unlikely that cars priced at £500 000 can be sold – but they are, because the individuals who buy them believe that they are worth the money. Thus, the benefits satisfy their needs. It may be assumed that the more expensive vehicle is, however, built, equipped and finished to higher tangible standards and probably provides higher intangible benefits to its purchaser, their most important needs probably being self-actualisation and esteem.

It is fair to say that 'you get what you pay for' and customers as a whole, subscribe to this view.

Competition and your customers

Very few firms have a monopoly. Even if they have a monopoly of a particular product or service, there is normally an alternative method of satisfying the need, e.g. British Rail Regions have a monopoly of railway services in their areas. However, buses, air travel and private cars offer alternative methods of satisfying the basic need – transport. So everybody faces competition and contrary to popular opinion it is not something to be frightened of.

Marketing sets out to study the competition and use this information in a positive way. The key is to develop a *differential advantage* over your competition, relevant to the needs of your target market. To do this you must:

- decide who your competitors are (local, national or international)
- understand customers' perceptions of the competition and their offerings
- collect as much information as possible, including advertisements, brochures, price lists, editorial copy and, if possible, published accounts

Following this, management needs to assess each competitor's strengths and weaknesses in line with the target audience's perceived needs. A convenient method of achieving this is presented in the following table comparing three tumble dryer products:

Product characteristic	Weight (or relative importance)	Brand A		Brand B		Brand C	
		Score	Weighted score	Score	Weighted score	Score	Weighted score
Capacity	7	6	42	7	49	6	42
Performance	6	8	48	4	24	2	12
Reliability	8	4	32	9	72	2	16
Indicators and controls	5	9	45	4	20	4	20
Convenience of use	3	9	27	2	6	7	21
			194		172		111

This table compares the three products (Brands A, B and C) on five product characteristics. This example suggests that a particular target audience has weighted these characteristics on a scale of 1–10 (1 = least important, 10 = most important) in terms of their importance to them.

The next stage is to get the same respondents to score *each* brand in terms of each characteristic, i.e. from bad = 1, to excellent = 10.

By multiplying the score by the weight we get a weighted score for each brand on each characteristic. These can be totalled to provide an overall score.

In the example, it appears that Brand A is perceived by the respondents as being the best product. The manager responsible for Brand B could improve its overall rating by increasing its score on the 'performance' characteristic (from 4 to 8).

This raises two points:

- If the physical product is inferior to Brand A on this characteristic, then steps need to be taken to rectify this.
- If, however, the products are broadly similar on this characteristic then it will be necessary to revise the promotional strategy to change the audience's perception of the product.

You will see that this is directly related to the 'targeting' problem illustrated by Figure 8 (page 35) which we looked at on Tuesday.

Summary

Customers perceive they have a need for a product or service and this perception is very much coloured by the customer's motives and personality.

Quite often customers have a hierarchy of needs (i.e. a list running from most important to least important) and marketers need to understand these hierarchies so that benefits can be matched to these needs.

Purchasing decisions may be made by more than one person, e.g. husband and wife; also, individuals are influenced by the views of 'significant' others.

It is important to distinguish between product *features* and product *benefits*. Product features produce benefits that can be matched to needs.

Both products and services have differing levels of tangible and intangible benefits. Intangible benefits such as feelings of exclusivity, etc. can sometimes be more important than the tangible benefits.

When customers are assessing different offerings they make value judgements, i.e. they consider the package of benefits offered by each product or service compared to their perceived needs and assess value in terms of how well the benefits match their needs at a particular cost – a benefit/cost trade off.

Competition is a fact of life and it is essential that competitive action is monitored and a close watch is kept on the customers' perceptions of our company and the competition.

Drafting the marketing strategy – an introduction

Now is a good time to recap. You have heard about the importance of considering the objectives for the business, the nature of the market and its segments.

Also, the needs and attitudes of the segments must be assessed, relative to the strengths and weaknesses of the competition.

We could have developed a strategy without going through these steps but the chances of failure would probably have been higher! This is where the matching process and the value of information in reducing risk in decision making come in. But we still haven't got a strategy, so to start with, what is a 'marketing strategy'?

A marketing strategy is a plan using the various marketing tools to achieve objectives in a marketing situation, i.e. it is a commitment of the future direction of the firm.

The substance of a marketing strategy can be divided into four areas, known as the marketing mix:–

- Product
- Price
- Distribution channels
- Promotion

All strategies have these four elements, but they are 'mixed' together differently.

This chapter will look at each marketing mix element in turn.

Product

The most important concern of a firm is the development of a viable product strategy. The product must have features that carry benefits (tangible and intangible) that are matched to the perceived needs of the target segment. These could be:

- The physical nature of the product – its style, colour, materials, etc., or its dimensions, capacity, performance
- The width of the range, i.e. the numbers of different products to be made, for example air vented tumble dyers, condenser type, and so on
- The depth of the range, i.e. how many different sizes or versions of the same product are going to be offered, e.g. full size or compacts

Price

We have touched on the concept of perceived value and here is a simple checklist for setting prices:

- What price does the competition set for similar products?
- Is there a discount structure?
- Do customers perceive our product as offering a better solution to their needs? If so, can we gauge how much more value, and hence, how much will they pay?
- What is the total variable cost of making the product?
- What would be the total cost at different levels of production?

Again, we can see the matching process. It is pointless selling a product at a price the customer perceives as good value if the total cost is above that price.

This approach can be represented graphically:

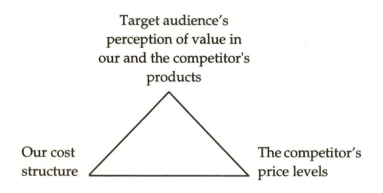

FIGURE 9   *The Pricing Triangle*

For instance, if the target audience perceives our product to be broadly similar in value to our competitor's then price becomes a sensitive issue. In other words, we cannot differentiate our product from theirs in terms of, say, quality.

Also, if a competitor prices the product at £20 and our total *variable* cost is £20 then we cannot enter this market under these conditions. Clearly, we would make a loss on every product we sold.

Distribution

There is a clear distinction between physical distribution – the delivery of goods to a customer – and the strategic selection of distribution *channels* to make the product/service available to the target market. In this section, we are concerned with the latter case.

Distribution channels are concerned with relationships between the producer, the *middleman* and the customer. In some markets, distribution is direct, i.e. there is no middleman. The producer sells direct to the end customer. Recent activity in many consumer markets has demonstrated growth in direct marketing through press direct response advertising, direct mailing and TV direct response advertising and even the Internet.

The channel chosen by a firm has an important effect on the other elements of the marketing mix. Product line, pricing and promotional decisions rest heavily on the type of distribution channel selected. This illustrates the interdependence of marketing strategy decisions.

There are five factors to be considered when deciding which channel to adopt.

- The size and distribution of the consumer market have a major bearing. For example, if the target market is concentrated amongst relatively few buyers within a limited geographical area, then the channels can be short (few middlemen between producer and customer).
- Product characteristics influence channel decisions. Such factors as perishability, complexity of assembly, seasonality, etc. all influence how the product is distributed.

- The nature of existing channels must be considered. Some wholesalers or retailers specialise in particular ranges of products relevant to particular target markets. Quite often, a small proportion of the outlets (say 20%) account for a large proportion (say 80%) of the sales. It is therefore important to identify which middlemen best reach your target market.

- Competitive activity must be considered. Some people are anxious to have their products in exactly the same 'point of sale' as their competitors. Others choose to adopt other channels that run parallel to their competitors' channels, e.g. direct marketing through the general press as an alternative distribution strategy to selling through traditional retail outlets.
- The position of the firm and its resources have a paramount importance in channel decisions. The scale of activity and position of the firm on its own growth curve dictate the parameters of these decisions. It is pointless considering international distribution strategies if manufacturing capacity is obviously below local demand levels.

Figure 10 presents a possible example of a distribution for tumble dryers:

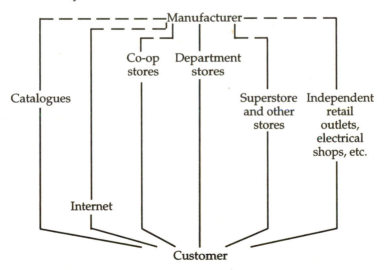

FIGURE 10 *Distribution Channels for Tumble Dryers*

Clearly, it would be valuable to know the shares of the market supplied by each channel and the trends in such shares over the last few years. For instance, catalogues may have a small share but may have grown rapidly and could be worth further consideration.

Also, it would be good to know how many organisations were involved in each channel. Probably, there would be fewer organisations in the department store channel than in the independent retail outlets channel. This could mean two things:

- Fewer customers would have a higher level of purchases and therefore targeting on the department stores would offer the best return on effort.
- But, having such purchasing power would make the department stores particularly strong.

Promotion

Everybody knows how to promote a product. Simply advertise it and wait for the orders to roll in! If only it were so simple. In this section we are going to look at five aspects of the promotional strategy.

- Setting promotional objectives
- Targeting
- Message design
- Media selection
- Evaluation

Setting promotional objectives
The purpose of the promotional strategy is to move the potential buyer from unawareness to buying action.

Russell Colley described the 'marketing communications spectrum' thus:

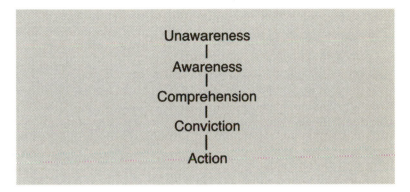

Unawareness
|
Awareness
|
Comprehension
|
Conviction
|
Action

It follows that promotional objectives should be set in terms of moving the target audience through these steps to the ultimate stage of 'action', i.e. buying the product or service.

Targeting
If the marketing strategy is developed in the way we have described, the firm will have a reasonable idea of who its potential customers are. In essence, the firm will have made a decision regarding which segment(s) to target and will have taken into consideration the customers' perceptions of the firm and the competition. The firm will have 'positioned' its product.

The more we know about the target audience, the easier it is to develop a promotional strategy because the knowledge of the following factors aids the development of appropriate responses:

- Characteristics of the target audience
- Hierarchy of needs
- Position on the marketing communications spectrum – 'Are they aware of us?'
- Readership habits
- Other external attitude influences

Message design

The message is a signal made up of words, pictures and sounds which collectively strive to impart one or more ideas, often through the use of *symbols.*

Messages can be classed as 'neutral' or 'persuasive'.

A *neutral* message is direct or descending rank (i.e. dealing with each point in turn) and tends to be concerned with imparting information. The tone is pleasant, concise and the content must be clear and complete. The action required from the audience is dated (e.g. 'sale starts Monday, ends Friday') and there is an opportunity for further information (e.g. a telephone number and/or address).

Persuasive messages tend to use the AIDA (Attention, Interest, Desire, Action) approach seeking to move the audience through these steps. The messages tend to have a strong creative element using images to help match benefits to perceived needs.

This approach can be used with any medium whether it be advertising or direct mail, etc.

Media selection
There are, of course, many ways of reaching our target audience. Media selection is about identifying those media which *best* reach our target audience. The key questions are:

- Whom does the medium reach?
- How many people will receive the message?
- What is the cost per 1000 people?

There is a wide range of available media, some of which are listed below:

National newspapers – Large, general audience, can be defined at a socio-economic level.

Regional newspapers – Smaller, more specific audiences at this geographical level.

Television – Audience is large and varies with time of day.

Radio (local) – Definable market, 'travel to work audiences' and general 'at home' audience.

Direct mail – Specifically targeted and therefore offering an opportunity to put a specific message to a group. Not always executed thoroughly and suffering from 'saturation nausea'.

Telephone selling	– Strong tool in business-to-business, also used for selling consumer durables like double glazing. Something of a compromise between direct mail and personal selling.
Internet	– Web sites online advertising, online buying and selling
Personal selling	– Probably the most effective (but most expensive) method of promotion. Personal selling offers the opportunity to ask questions and present benefits *specific* to that customer. For many products, personal selling is essential to the final stage of the process, i.e. action. A classic example is car sales.
Public relations	– Requires detailed planning and implementation to establish and maintain a mutual understanding between the organisation and its publics.

Evaluation

Clearly the most important result of promotional activity is a sale. However, the link between promotion (particularly advertising) and sales is too tenuous, complicated and long-term to permit measuring the direct impact. A better way to measure effectiveness is to use marketing research at pre (before the campaign) and post (after the campaign) stages to measure that change in attitude on behalf of the target group attributable to a particular promotional activity.

Summary

Marketing strategy is a plan using the various marketing tools to achieve objectives in a marketing situation. There are four main areas known as the *marketing mix*:

Product — this refers to the features that carry benefits to the customer.

Price — setting prices is a separate exercise from costing. Prices need to be set in terms of the customers' price: value assessment of the product. In doing this, competitive action must be considered.

Distribution — this refers to the selection of distribution channels, i.e. ways of making the product available to the target audience.

Promotion — promoting a product involves *informing* and *persuading* customers to buy. Customers move through a series of attitudinal stages (unaware – aware, etc.) before they buy and marketers must set promotional objectives and strategies to accomplish 'moving' the audience through these stages. Media used in conveying the messages will need to be selected on the basis of which reach the audience and levels of effectiveness at different attitudinal stages.

Review

Remember that we live in a dynamic world. Our world is changing politcally, economically, culturally and technologically – the only constant is change!

Quite clearly, a marketing strategy needs regular review. Budgets and forecasts help the business monitor performance, but we also need to observe trends outside the business, in the marketplace and in the economy and society generally.

A major problem in marketing is getting lost in the tactics of a plan and occasionally going off course. Regular review helps to avoid this trap.

It is worth reviewing our objectives:

- Are they now relevant to the state of the firm?
- Are the markets and segments changing, which will mean a change in the firm's strategy?

Marketing, to a great extent, is applied common sense, augmented by certain techniques and knowledge, borrowed from other disciplines.

The key is to remember that our customers dictate whether we survive or not. We do not have a right to their money, we must earn it. Marketing's task is to match the skills and resources of the firm to the needs and wants of the marketplace.

Your checklist

This checklist is based on the marketing decision process (see Figure 3, page 16) and is designed to help you apply this concept to your business. The steps have been ordered to follow a logical flow and you will appreciate that they are interrelated.

- What are our objectives for the business?
- How can we state these in qualitative and quantitative terms?
- What are our strengths and weaknesses?
- What are our marketing goals?
- What is the nature of our marketplace (size, trends, etc.)?
- How can the market be segmented?
- Who are our competitors and what are their strengths and weaknesses?
- What are the needs of the various market segments and how do they perceive the benefits in our product?
- How do they perceive the benefits of our competitors' products?
- Are our marketing goals realistic in terms of the opportunities and threats in the marketplace?
- Which segment offers the best match of our strengths to their perceived needs – i.e. what is/are our target/s?
- What benefits, tangible and intangible, does our product need to have to be perceived as having a differential advantage over our competition?
- What is the target segment's perception of value – i.e. what package of benefits most closely meets their needs at the best price? How will we price to ensure

the ratio of benefits: price (i.e. the value ratio) is right for the target?

- What are the current channels of distribution for this segment?
- What are the trends in distribution channel share for the market?
- Where can we place our product for maximum effect, i.e. to maximise our strengths and minimise those of our competitors?
- What is our target audience's behaviour in terms of exposure to media, visiting exhibitions, attitudes to direct mail, etc.?
- Where on the attitudinal spectrum do we think the majority of our audience is?
- What is going to be our message platform – neutral or persuasive (or both)?
- How are we going to make the message platform operational, i.e. the use of copy and images, format for different media, etc.?
- Which media reach our target audience?
- Which media offer the best reach at the lowest cost?
- When should we schedule our promotions?
- How are we going to monitor the performance of our promotional activity (pre- and post-studies of attitudes)?
- How are we going to measure the overall effect of our marketing strategies (i.e. for each marketing mix element)? Do we opt for internal analysis of sales and profit, research into customer perceptions and behaviour or performance of competitors?
- How are we going to ensure that our plan is updated to reflect changes in the environment?

Summary

Marketing is a body of knowledge concerned with the relationship of a business to its market place. Many readers will be familiar with TQM, (Total Quality Management), as an approach to creating 'customer-driven' companies. 'Quality', in this context, can be defined as 'conforming to customer requirements', and this establishes the strong link between marketing and TQM. In essence, to be successful in a modern, highly competitive business environment, a business needs to be truly customer-focused (or oriented), and this means the entire business – not just one department.

The world is a dynamic place, and the rate of change is increasing – it is essential that businesses have 'heightened environmental sensitivity' to watch for new opportunities and threats. But, perhaps more importantly, firms need to be *genuinely marketing orientated* and prepared to adapt to meet the new needs. Those who do not are more likely to fail than those who do.